A RIOT OF
IRISH WRITERS
A Romp Through Irish Literature

D1505622

A RIOT OF IRISH WRITERS

A Romp Through Irish Literature

TERRANCE DICKS
Illustrated by RAY JELLIFFE

Piccadilly Press · London

Phototypeset by Goodfellow & Egan, Cambridge
Printed and bound by Hartnolls Ltd., Bodmin
for the publishers, Piccadilly Press Ltd.,
5 Castle Road, London NW1 8PR

A catalogue record for this book is available
from the British Library

ISBN 1-85340-184-6 (hardback)
ISBN 1-85340-173-0 (trade paperback)

Terrance Dicks is British and lives in North London with his wife and three
sons. A very well-known author, he has written over a hundred books for
children including the following series for Piccadilly Press: *The Adventures
of David & Goliath*, *Jonathan's Ghost*, *A Cat Called Max*, and *The MacMagics*.
Piccadilly Press published his *Europe United* and very recently,
A Riot of Writers.

Ray Jelliffe is British and lives in Berkshire with his wife. Now retired, but
working harder than ever, he used to be a creative director of a large
advertising agency. He has illustrated numerous greeting cards and several
books, including *Europe United* and *A Riot of Writers*.

Contents

Introduction

Harry Lime, in 'The Third Man', points out that while Italy's turbulent history produced great art by the cart-load, Switzerland, after years of peace and prosperity, came up with – the cuckoo clock!

The literary history of Ireland seems to support Harry's theory. If Ireland has had more than its share of historical mayhem and political turmoil, it has also produced an amazingly high proportion of the world's greatest writers.

As you might expect, most of them were rebels in one way and another, rejecting all forms of established authority. Quite a few spent some time as what Frank O'Connor tactfully calls 'Guests of the State'.

Many were lifelong exiles.

Nevertheless, Ireland made them and shaped them and they never forgot their native land.

So here they are, a round dozen of Irish writers. From Jonathan Swift to Seamus Heaney, they're amazing, original and often outrageous – but never dull!

'Bred any good rooks lately?'

Chapter One

JONATHAN SWIFT
1667–1745

Satirical Swift

Swift is one of those writers who wrote a book *everyone* knows. Such success can be a bit of a mixed blessing. The fame of 'Gulliver's Travels' overshadows the rest of Swift's life and work. It's a pity because Swift is one of literature's most interesting and complex characters. A rather reluctant churchman, he was fond of the ladies and heavily involved in politics. He was always grumbling about Ireland – and forever fighting for its interests. He was a fine poet, and a blisteringly effective political satirist whose work made Governments tremble.

'I see Swift's blisteringly effective satire has made the Government tremble again!'

Although he never married, he conducted a lifelong romance with a lady he called Stella.

Jonathan Swift was born in Dublin in 1667. His father, an English

1

lawyer, died before he was born, and a few years later his mother went back to her native Leicestershire, leaving little Jonathan in the care of his uncle, Godwin.

Swift was educated at Kilkenny School and went on to Trinity College, Dublin. He didn't think much of the place and the feeling seems to have been mutual. After several disputes with college authorities, Swift finally graduated 'speciale gratia' – the kind of pass that's one jump ahead of a fail.

Home to Mum

In 1689 the English chucked out their Catholic king, James II, who promptly came over to Ireland and raised an army. Fighting broke out everywhere, and Swift decided it was time he visited Mum in England. Through family influence he got a job as private secretary to a diplomat called Sir William Temple. Swift lived at Sir William's country house, Moor Park, for several years. Amongst his other duties he acted as tutor to a little girl called Esther Johnson, the child of Sir William's sister's companion. Years later, when Esther had grown up into a beautiful young woman, she became the love of his life, immortalised in his work, under the name of Stella.

Poetry and Politics

Swift wrote a number of poems around this time, but early reaction wasn't exactly encouraging. His cousin Dryden, top playwright of the day, said dismissively, 'Cousin Swift, you will never be a poet!' Perhaps fortunately, Swift wasn't pinning all his hopes on poetry. He had high hopes that his job with Sir William would lead on to a career in politics and his master employed him on a number of high-powered diplomatic missions. But somehow the promised advancement never arrived. Disillusioned, Swift returned to

Ireland and took Holy Orders in the Anglican Church. After two years in Ireland, he came back to Moor Park where he wrote a couple of satires, 'The Tale of a Tub' and 'The Battle of the Books'.

Sir William Temple died in 1699 and Swift, deprived of his patron, went back to Ireland, where he became chaplain to the Earl of Berkeley. In 1791 he became attached to St Patrick's Cathedral. Later he became Vicar of Laracor in County Meath.

Swift and Stella

He'd kept up his correspondence with his Stella all this time and she eventually moved to Dublin with a female friend as chaperone. Swift and Stella met constantly in the years that followed – but, as far as anyone knew, they were never alone together. Their relationship is one of literature's big mysteries. They were certainly devoted to each other – but no-one knows whether their affection was platonic, semi-platonic, or led to a full-scale affair. (It's true Swift was a clergyman, but naughty priests weren't unknown in those days – it's all quite different today of course!) There's even a rumour they

'Oh stella – the pillar of the Church comes between us!'

were secretly married – but no-one knows for sure. Swift was back in England on church business between 1710 and 1714 and a collection of his letters to her, 'Journal to Stella', was published after his death.

Swift Settles Down

Despite his sterling services to the church, Swift never got on as well in public life as he'd hoped. Some of his satire got up the nose of Queen Anne, and she blocked his advancement.

But he didn't do too badly in the end, returning to Ireland as Dean of St Patrick's in 1713. From now on he was to be based largely in Dublin. Although he never stopped grumbling about Ireland, he became a tireless worker for Irish rights, writing a number of savagely effective political pamphlets. One, 'A Letter to the Whole People of Ireland', attacked a fiendish English scheme to debase Irish currency. The pamphlet was anonymous and the enraged Government offered a big reward for the capture of the writer. Everyone in Dublin knew it was Swift, but nobody talked. The plan collapsed and he became a public hero.

Gulliver's Travels

In 1720 Swift started writing 'Gulliver's Travels', his most famous work and the only one for which he ever got paid. 'Gulliver's Travels' is really several books. Lemuel Gulliver, a very unlucky sailor, gets shipwrecked on every voyage. In Book I he lands up in Lilliput where people are only six inches high. It's this book people remember best, with the giant Gulliver tied down on the beach by an army of six-inch soldiers . . .

'Gawd — I've been clamped!'

Gentle Giants, Mad Scientists, Wise Horses

In Book II the tables are turned. Gulliver arrives in Brobdingnag where the people are all giants, and the tiny Gulliver an interesting freak.

In Book III Gulliver visits the flying island of Laputa and meets its mad philosophers. On nearby Lagado he sees equally mad scientists, working to breed wool-less sheep and extract sunshine from cucumbers. He meets the terrifying Strudlbruggs, who grow more and more decayed but can never die . . .

In Book IV Gulliver goes to the land of the Houyhnhums, intelligent and noble horses ruling debased and bestial humans.

'Mother, exactly how friendly were you with Gulliver?'

Gulliver's Satire

Swift's aim in all four books was to satirise the vices and follies of mankind, like going to war over trifles. In Lilliput there's a war between 'Big-Endians' and 'Little-Endians' – those who believe you

should crack a
boiled egg at the big end, and
those who insist on attacking
the smaller.

When Gulliver boasts to the
giant king of Brobdingnag of
mankind's weapons of destruction,
the horrified king says:

> *'I cannot*
> *but conclude the Bulk of your*
> *Natives to be the most pernicious*
> *Race of little odious Vermin that*
> *Nature ever suffered to crawl*
> *upon the surface of this Earth.'*

In reality Swift was a kind-hearted man, aroused to indignation by
the injustice and cruelty of mankind in the mass.

> *'I hate and detest that animal called man: although I heartily love John,*
> *Peter, Thomas and so forth . . .'*

A Modest Proposal
One of his most savage works was produced in his later years. Called
'A Modest Proposal for Preventing the Children of Poor People
from Being a Burden', it suggested a simple solution – use them for
food!

'A young healthy child well nursed is at a year old a most delicious, nourishing and wholesome food whether stewed, roasted, baked or boiled . . .'

It was Swift's message to Ireland's English rulers. Their uncaring policies were already killing children. Why not go the whole hog and eat them as well? It's still a blood-curdlingly effective piece of political satire.

Swift died in 1745 and was buried in St Patrick's next to his beloved Stella who had died twelve years earlier.

'Here lies Swift,' says his epitaph, 'where savage indignation can no longer tear his heart . . .'

Swift however had already provided his own epitaph.

In his poem 'On the Death of Dr Swift' he wrote:

'Yet malice never was his aim
He lashed the vice but spared the name
No individual could resent
Where thousands equally were meant . . .'

Chapter Two

OSCAR WILDE
1854–1900

Oscar the Great
Oscar Wilde – Oscar Fingal O'Flahertie Wills Wilde to give him his full name – was born in Dublin, the son of a successful surgeon, Sir William Wilde. His mum gave literary parties and wrote revolutionary poetry.

A high-flyer from the start, Oscar was educated at Trinity College, Dublin, and at Magdalen College, Oxford, where he won the Newdigate Prize for poetry and took a first-class degree.

Oscar Goes to Town
Oscar arrived in London with a ready-made reputation as a wit and poet. He dressed outrageously, talked flamboyantly, collected peacock's feathers and declared himself a believer in 'Art for Art's sake'.

A wild Irishman sneaked up behind me and pinched my feathers

That was Wilde

He was what was known as an aesthete – the sort of young man who turns up today in arts programmes on the telly. In 1881 he published a volume of poetry, and by 1882 he was off on a lecture tour of America. Going through American Customs he was asked if he had anything to declare. 'I have nothing to declare except my genius,' said Oscar loftily.

Wilde enjoyed America. Writing about a Western town called Leadville, in his 'Impressions of America', he described a bar-room notice:

'Please do not shoot the pianist. He is doing his best.'

Oscar Settles Down

Soon after that, you may be surprised to learn, he married a lady called Constance Lloyd – they had two sons. He became the editor of a magazine, 'Woman's World'. He produced a book of fairy tales (no jokes please) called 'The Happy Prince'. He wrote a book of short stories 'Lord Arthur Savile's Crime' and his one and only novel, 'The Picture of Dorian Grey.' It's the story of a handsome but evil young man who *stays* young and handsome – despite years and years spent in every kind of wickedness and debauchery. Turns out he's got this picture of himself in his attic. Dorian doesn't change, but the picture

gets older and more evil every day. In the preface, Oscar spells out his artistic creed:

'There is no such thing as a moral or an immoral book. Books are well written or badly written.'

Oscar On Stage

Oscar's first attempts at drama, tragedies like 'Vera, or the Nihilists' and 'The Duchess of Padua' were all flops. Even the highly-coloured 'Salome' didn't do too well, though the famous Dance of the Seven Veils caused quite a scandal. Oscar tried another approach. Over the following years, he produced a string of brilliantly successful social comedies.

Lady Windermere and Others

In the first, 'Lady Windermere's Fan' there are such gems as:

'I can resist everything except temptation,'

and Oscar's famous definition of a cynic:

'A man who knows the price of everything, and the value of nothing.'

'A Woman of No Importance' has another famous definition, much quoted by today's anti-hunting lobby:

'The English country gentleman galloping after a fox – the unspeakable in full pursuit of the uneatable.'

The Importance of Being Earnest

The funniest, the most-successful and the most famous of all Oscar's plays, 'The Importance of Being Earnest' is still frequently read and performed today. Even the title is a joke. The heroine says she could never love a man unless his name was Ernest – which is tough on the hero, who thinks his name is Jack. (Luckily it turns out to be Ernest after all.) His girl-friend's mother, the formidable Lady Bracknell is far from pleased to learn that he's an orphan:

'To lose one parent, Mr Worthing, may be regarded as a misfortune; to lose both looks like carelessness.'

It doesn't help matters much when Jack explains that as a baby he was found in a handbag in a station cloakroom.

Lady Bracknell: *A handbag!*

(As delivered by Dame Edith Evans, and by a variety of other famous actresses, this two-word line is the biggest sure-fire laugh in the history of the theatre.)

Oscar's Downfall

So far Oscar's life sounds like one long success story. But, of course, he had a secret. He was gay or, strictly speaking, bisexual. Today it simply wouldn't matter much. Then, things were very different. Homosexuality was still a crime. It was possible to stay out of trouble by being discreet. But Oscar was colourful, flamboyant and openly camp. Worse still, he had a powerful enemy. One of Oscar's many fashionable friends was a young man called Lord Alfred Douglas, commonly known as Bosie. Bosie's father was the Marquess of Queensberry, a huntin', shootin' and fishin' peer of the old school, and bonkers into the bargain. Convinced that Oscar Wilde had seduced and corrupted his son, the Marquess set out to destroy him.

Oscar in Court

For a time Oscar ignored the Marquess's taunts, but when an insulting note was left at his club, Oscar sued the Marquess for libel. It was a fatal mistake. Oscar was up against the Establishment in full force, and his witty quips didn't go down too well in the dock. He lost the case. Shortly afterwards, Oscar was prosecuted 'for homosexual offences' and sentenced to two years' hard labour. He left a

'Prison food's so awful, it can make you feel queer!'

moving record of his suffering in his famous poem, 'The Ballad of Reading Gaol':

*'I know not whether Laws be right
Or whether Laws be wrong;
All that we know who live in gaol*

Is that the walls are strong;
And that each day is like a year,
A year whose days are long.'

Wilde felt betrayed by his friends. The poem's tone is bitter:

'Yet each man kills the thing he loves,
By each let this be heard,
Some do it with a bitter look,
Some with a flattering word.
The coward does it with a kiss,
The brave man with a sword!'

On his release Wilde went to France, where he struggled with poverty and poor health for three more years (his wife stayed in England, didn't divorce him, but changed her name). Wilde was defiantly witty to the last: 'Paris has always been an expensive place to die,' he complained. 'Particularly for a foreigner . . .'

Presented with a big medical bill on his deathbed he said, 'I suppose that I shall have to die beyond my means . . .'

It is also said that his last words as he gazed at the hotel wallpaper were: 'Either it goes, or I go,' and he promptly died.

Oscar Wilde died in disgrace, in poverty and in exile. It was a sad end to a glittering career. But as long as somewhere on some stage an outraged Lady Bracknell exclaims, 'A handbag!' and the theatre explodes with laughter, poor old Oscar Wilde will never be entirely forgotten . . .

Chapter Three

GEORGE BERNARD SHAW
1856–1950

George Bernard Shaw was born in a Protestant family in Dublin, the son of a boozy dad and a musical mum. When Shaw was sixteen, his mother got fed up with waiting for dad to come home from the pub and made off to London with her two daughters. Shaw, who was working for a firm of land agents, stayed on in Ireland a few years longer. When he was twenty, he threw up his job and joined his mother and sisters in London, determined to become a writer.

He started by writing five novels, all flops. (Shaw himself reckoned he earned about nine quid in his first ten years as an author.) At the same time he was working hard to educate himself. He read Karl

'I've heard of GBH but what's GBS?'

Marx and became a life-long socialist. Naturally shy, he joined the Fabian Society, an early group of socialist intellectuals, and made himself into a brilliant public speaker. With his mother's help, he gradually built up a career as a music critic, writing under the unlikely name of Corno di Bassetto.

Shaw Takes the Stage

He became a theatre critic too, much influenced by the modern ideas of Norwegian playwright Henrik Ibsen. Shaw soon became disillusioned with the artificiality of the London stage, and decided he could do better. He was never exactly overburdened with modesty. In a later essay he wrote:

'With the single exception of Homer, there is no eminent writer, not even Sir Walter Scott, whom I can despise so entirely as I despise Shakespeare when I measure my mind against his.'

Shaw started writing a new kind of play – the play of ideas. Each of his plays deals with at least one big central theme.

Plays of Ideas

Shaw's first play, 'Widowers' Houses' is about the corruptions of capitalism. A Victorian gent is faced with the fact that the money which makes him rich and respectable comes from the rents on slum properties.

His next play, 'Mrs Warren's Profession' dealt with society's sexual hypocrisy, and the ethics of prostitution. This time he'd gone too far. Banned for the next ten years, the play wasn't actually staged until 1902. Undeterred Shaw went on writing in exactly the same style.

'Arms and the Man' deals with the reality as opposed to the myth of war. Its hero, Bluntschli is more concerned with scrounging food and staying alive than with death or glory.

'You can always tell an old soldier . . . The young ones carry pistols and cartridges, the old ones grub.'

THE CHOCOLATE SOLDIER

Bluntschli himself keeps his ammunition pouches filled with chocolate. (The play was made into a successful musical – called 'The Chocolate Soldier'!)

Shaw's Fair Lady

A later play, 'Pygmalion' dealt with the English class system, and the way we judge people by the way they talk. Perhaps the most popular of Shaw's plays, it tells how the arrogant Professor Higgins makes a bet that he can teach flower girl Eliza Doolittle to talk like a lady:

> *'Remember that you are a human being with a soul and the divine gift of articulate speech . . .'* he tells the baffled Eliza. *'Don't sit there crooning like a bilious pigeon!'*

Like many of Shaw's plays, 'Pygmalion' was successfully filmed. Later it was made into a hit musical, 'My Fair Lady'.

'Do yer reckon yer better than Berlitz?'

Shaw the Feminist

Many of Shaw's plays feature strong independent women – a pretty daring idea in those days. (When he started writing, women didn't even have the vote.) 'Caesar and Cleopatra' shows the young and impulsive Cleopatra being turned into a real queen by the older and wiser Julius Caesar, who teaches her to rule:

> *'Without punishment. Without revenge. Without judgement.'*

'Haven't seen much of your "Life Force" lately Emma!'

Other plays like 'Candida', 'Saint Joan' and his Salvation Army play, 'Major Barbara' all feature strong, independent-minded heroines. Shaw believed in something he called the Life Force, the blind power of evolution working through man. He saw women as the real carriers of this mysterious force. In most of his plays, they are stronger and more determined than the men. In 'Man and Superman' the revolutionary and would-be free spirit Tanner says:

> *'It is a woman's business to get married as soon as possible, and a man's to keep unmarried as long as he can.'*

But the determined heroine, Ann, gets him in the end. She's got the Life Force on her side.

A Load of (Brilliant) Old Chat

Shaw covered every subject under the sun in his plays, from Irish politics in 'John Bull's Other Island' to medical ethics in 'The Doctor's Dilemma'. He was fascinated by ideas of every kind, political, philosophical, and even religious. Not a lot actually happens in his plays. Mostly people just stand around and argue. This could have made for a lot of amazingly boring message plays – but Shaw is anything but boring. Luckily for him, and for us, he was a born dramatist with a strong comic sense. He creates wonderful characters and writes hilariously comic scenes. His bad characters get even better lines than his good ones. In 'Pygmalion' Eliza's disreputable father says:

> *'I'm one of the* undeserving *poor, that's what I am. Think what that means to a man . . . he's up agen middle class mortality all the time.'*

Public Shaw

Over the years, Shaw slowly turned into a celebrity. He was active in politics and he wrote and lectured endlessly. The tall thin bearded figure popped up everywhere. He visited the front in the First World War, won the Nobel Prize for Literature in 1925, visited Stalin's Russia in 1931, and survived to see World War Two, the defeat of Hitler, the post-war Labour Government, and the start of the NHS.

Shaw in Private

There's not much to say about Shaw's private life – largely because he didn't really have one. He lived his life on stage, in the public eye, and he was only really interested in ideas. A lifelong vegetarian and teetotaller, he didn't seem to have any vices at all. (Nudge, nudge, wink, wink, know what I mean?) There were lots of adoring lady disciples, and flirtations with society hostesses and famous actresses – but Shaw kept everything firmly on the mental plane.

When he was ill in 1898 an Irish heiress called Charlotte moved in to look after him. Shaw married her to avoid a scandal and they lived happily but platonically together for the next forty-five years.

'Do you take this woman to cook and to clean...?'

The Grandest Old Man

George Bernard Shaw lived to the amazing age of ninety-four – there must be something in this vegetarian lark after all. He kept on writing almost to the end, publishing 'Everybody's Political What's What' when he was over ninety. Busy and active to the last, he was pruning trees in his garden when he had a fall. He died on November 2nd 1950, one of the grandest, and certainly the oldest, of Eng Lit's Grand Old Men.

Chapter Four

WILLIAM BUTLER YEATS
1865–1939

A Sword Upstairs

Yeats had two great passions, Ireland and poetry, and he believed passionately in both:

'When I was young
I had not given a penny for a song
Did not the poet sing it with such airs
That one believed he had a sword upstairs.'

Yeats was born in Dublin into a highly artistic family. His father and his brother were both painters. Yeats himself studied at the School

Mother come and see
— William's done another
abstract!

of Art in Dublin for three years. He developed an intense interest in mysticism and the supernatural, and was asked to leave the Theosophical Society for over-enthusiastic experiments!

Lost in the Celtic Twilight

It was the time of the Irish literary revival, and Yeats turned from art to literature. He studied Ireland's ancient Celtic mythology, writing prose works like 'The Land of Heart's Desire'.

'Your Supernatural pursuits have come to our notice — you'll have to leave!'

'The land of faery
Where nobody gets old and godly and grave,
Where nobody gets old and crafty and wise
Where nobody gets old and bitter of tongue.'

He edited an edition of the poems of William Blake and founded an Irish Literary Society, first in London and then in Dublin. He also fell madly in love with a beautiful Irish actress called Maud Gonne. A fierce revolutionary, Maud turned down his proposals of marriage, providing young Yeats with two things every poet needs – a cause to fight for and an unhappy love affair.

'All things uncomely and broken, all things worn out and old,
The cry of a child by the roadway, the creak of a lumbering cart,
The heavy steps of the ploughman, splashing the wintry mould
Are wronging your image that blossoms, a rose in the deeps of my heart.'

On Stage Please

In 1897 Yeats met Lady Gregory. A dramatist and a patron of literature, she aroused his interest in the theatre. He became one of the founders of the Irish Literary Theatre, which became, in 1902, the Irish National Dramatic Society. One of its first productions was 'Cathleen ni Houlihan', a romantic play about the struggle for Irish independence. It was written by Yeats and starred, of course, the lovely Maud. But when Yeats proposed Maud still said no. Worse still, in 1903 she got married to a fellow-revolutionary.

In 1905 Yeats was a founder of Dublin's famous Abbey Theatre. His tragedy 'Deirdre' was performed there in 1906. In 1913 he met the eccentric English poet Ezra Pound who became his secretary – and fencing master. (Yeats was obviously serious about that sword!) Between bouts, Ezra introduced Yeats to the Noh Plays of the

Japanese theatre which became a major influence on his work. Later Yeats wrote:

'I thought no more was needed
Youth to prolong
Than dumb-bell and foil
To keep the body young.
Oh who could have foretold
That the heart grows old?'

The Easter Rising

In 1916 came the heroic but ill-timed Easter Rising. It was suppressed after five days, and many of the leaders were executed.

Yeats was out of Ireland at the time, but many of the executed revolutionaries were his friends. The Rising made a great impression on Yeats, renewing his faith in the heroic nature of his country:

'All changed, changed utterly:
'A terrible beauty is born.'

Marriage and Mysticism

One of the executed leaders was Maud Gonne's husband.

After a tactful interval, Yeats proposed again, and again Maud said no. Deciding to keep things in the family, he proposed to her grown-up daughter, the illegitimate child of Maud's earlier affair with a Frenchman. She turned him down too. Fed up, Yeats married a long time girlfriend called Georgie Hyde Lees. She had the mystic power of automatic writing (in which some spirit guides the writer's hand) and demonstrated her gift on their honeymoon. (Well, you've got to pass the time somehow, haven't you?) Strangely enough, this performance inspired Yeats to resume writing poetry.

'Do Automatic writers have fax numbers?'

He produced a number of important collections, including 'A Vision', 'The Tower' and 'The Winding Stair'.

A Warm Welcome

After his marriage Yeats lived in Oxford then returned to Dublin in 1922. The troubles were in full swing and he had a warm welcome home. The bridge at his country house was blown up, and shots were fired into his home. Next year things went better – Yeats became a Senator, and won the Nobel Prize for Literature.

Yeats continued writing fine poetry and plays and his work influenced many modern poets. His health started to fail him in later life and in 1939 when he was spending the winter in the south of France he died. He was buried there in Roquebrune, but after the war it was felt that Ireland's greatest poet should be buried in Ireland. He was dug up and re-buried in Sligo in 1948 – at least that was the idea. There may have been some mix-up about the bones. We can only hope that most of him made it safely home to his beloved Ireland.

A Poet of Today

Yeats's work spans an incredibly wide range, including journalism, plays, poetry and prose. His later poetry was very different from his earlier work. Instead of being lush and romantic it was dry, witty and frequently laconic, using strong rhythms and simple, highly-condensed language. The poetry takes a philosophical, sometimes cynical view of life and love, and is often despairing about humanity and its future.

'Nor dread nor hope attend
A dying animal
A man awaits his end
Dreading and hoping all . . .'

But there was also a sort of defiant cheerfulness.

'An aged man is but a paltry thing,
A tattered coat upon a stick, unless,
Soul clap its hands and sing and louder sing,
For every tatter in its mortal dress.'

Yeats is best remembered for two of his gentler lyrics. One is a tribute to a lifelong love:

'When you are old and gray and full of sleep
And nodding by the fire, take down this book
And slowly read, and dream of the soft look
Your eyes had once, and of their shadows deep.
How many loved your moments of glad grace
And loved your beauty with love false or true
But one man loved the pilgrim soul in you
And loved the sorrows of your changing face . . .'

The other depicts everyone's longing to get away from it all:

'I will arise and go now, and go to Innisfree
And a small cabin build there, of clay and wattles made . . .
Nine bean rows will I have there, a hive for the honey bee,
And live alone in the bee-loud glade . . .
And I shall have some peace there, for peace comes dropping slow
Dropping from the veils of the morning to where the cricket
   sings.'

Like Swift, Yeats wrote his own epitaph:

'Under bare Ben Bulben's head
In Drumcliff churchyard, Yeats is laid
On limestone quarried near the spot
By his command, these words are cut:
"Cast a cold eye
On life, on death,
Horseman, pass by!"'

Chapter Five

SEAN O'CASEY
1880–1964

Heroic Outsider

Sean O'Casey was an outsider from the very first. He was born John
O'Casey in Dublin, youngest of a family of thirteen children. He was
an outsider because his family were Protestants in largely Catholic
Dublin. He was doubly an outsider because they were *poor* Protestants, in a country where, most Protestants were prosperous.

A Late Beginning

Young John grew up in Dublin's tenements against a background of
grinding poverty. He was pretty lucky to grow up at all – his father
died when he was six and only five of his thirteen brothers and
sisters survived. As a child he suffered from an eye disease. He
couldn't go to school and there was a danger that he would go blind.

'He's going to a poor Protestant family of 13 brothers and sisters!'

'And they talk of the luck of the Irish!'

Young John was a fighter and somehow he survived all his troubles. His eyesight improved and he learned to read – taught by his sister when he was fourteen years old. Once he started to read he never stopped. He fell in love with literature and in particular, with the works of Shakespeare. Supporting himself by a series of labouring jobs, he educated himself by reading all the books he could beg, borrow,

or occasionally steal. He developed an over-riding ambition – to become a writer, and to have a play staged at Dublin's famous Abbey Theatre.

Plays and Politics

John O'Casey grew up in a time of fierce political activity. He became a fighting socialist and a dedicated Irish nationalist as well, joining a number of increasingly revolutionary societies. He learned Irish and changed his name to Sean O'Cathasaigh – though he later compromised on Sean O'Casey. He began writing plays, and after years of effort he achieved his ambition. His first four submissions were rejected – but in 1923, when the forty-four-year-old O'Casey was working as a builder's labourer, 'The Shadow of a Gunman' was staged at the Abbey Theatre. Very much a play of its time, it was a romantic tragedy.

'They're on their way to the Abbey Theatre
– there's an O'Casey play on tonight!'

The hero is a poet, mistaken for a revolutionary on the run. The heroine saves him by taking some bombs left in his room – and is shot by British Irregular troops, the notorious Black and Tans.

Juno and the Paycock

The play was a success, and O'Casey lost no time in writing another. It was called 'Juno and the Paycock'. More realistic than the first, it tells the story of an impoverished Dublin family, the Boyles. 'Juno' is the mother, who holds the family together. The 'Paycock' is her husband, the strutting boasting 'Captain' Boyle. Juno is the family's sole support. Her son Johnny has lost an arm in the revolution, her left-wing trade-unionist daughter Mary is out on strike and her husband Boyle is too idle and too drunken to work.

The Boyles become suddenly rich, thanks to an unexpected legacy – and are plunged back into poverty when the will turns out to be faulty.

Tragedy strikes when Juno's beloved son Johnny turns out to be not a hero but a traitor. He has betrayed a comrade, and two Republican 'Irregulars' come to take him away to execution. Mary has become pregnant by her new lover, a school teacher who abandons her. When he hears the news, her first sweetheart, a young trade-union leader, abandons her as well.

'A terrible state o' chassis'

When Juno learns Boyle knew the will was faulty and went on spending anyway she comes to the end of her patience.

'I've done all I could an' it was no use – he'll be hopeless till the end of his days.'

She takes her daughter Mary and goes off to start a new life. She says:

'My poor little child that'll have no father.'

The indomitable Juno, a feminist before her time, says,

'It'll have what's far betther – it'll have two mothers.'

After they leave, Boyle and his boozing mate Joxer stagger back from the pub. Too drunk to realise that not only his furniture but his family have gone, Boyle drunkenly delivers the play's most famous line:

'Th' whole worl's in a terrible state o' chassis.'

Trouble at the Abbey

The play was a huge success and ran for a whole two weeks, helping to save the ever-rocky finances of the theatre. With a magnificent £25 in royalties in his pocket, O'Casey became a full-time writer – and ran straight into trouble.

His next play, 'The Plough and the Stars', was staged by the Abbey Theatre in 1926. It was set in the Easter Rising of 1916, an almost sacred event in the mind of Irish patriots everywhere. But O'Casey saw the bloodshed of the revolution as something far from noble and heroic. Against a background of inspiring patriotic speeches he showed ordinary people being killed, losing their children, being driven mad by suffering. Nor does their suffering make them noble. Some are capable of looting and stealing, and one of the characters is a prostitute . . .

The patriotic Abbey audience was outraged and there were riots and storms of protest. The poet and playwright Yeats, one of the Abbey's founders, defended O'Casey against his attackers. 'You have disgraced yourselves again,' he told them sternly. 'Dublin has once more rocked the cradle of genius. The fame of O'Casey is born here tonight.'

O'Casey Clears Off

But the audiences wouldn't listen and the boos and hisses continued. While his fellow-Irishmen were hurling brickbats at O'Casey, the cunning English chose this moment to award him the Hawthornden Prize for literature. The offended O'Casey decided to go where he was appreciated and went off to England to accept the prize. Soon afterwards he married a young Irish actress, and settled in England more or less permanently. Like many another Irish writer, he became an exile.

It was Ireland's loss and, as it turned out, O'Casey's as well. The move cut him off from the rich and colourful Dublin life that had provided his best material, and ended his useful working relationship with the Abbey Theatre. To make matters worse, the Abbey rejected his next play, 'The Silver Tassie'. This was about a wounded footballer, a British soldier in the First World War, who loses his beloved to his best friend. The second act, depicting the fighting at the front, was largely surrealist. Yeats ticked O'Casey off for abandoning both Irish subjects and theatrical realism – a bit much when you consider Yeats had written some pretty unrealistic plays himself.

(The play was eventually put on at the Abbey in 1935. It ran for a week, and was condemned for being immoral.)

O'Casey in Exile

O'Casey spent the rest of his life in England, eventually settling down in Devon. He continued writing plays, many of them experimental and expressionist in character. Two of his later plays, 'The Bishop's Bonfire' and 'The Drums of Father Ned', aroused more controversy in Ireland. The second was censored, and the enraged O'Casey banned all performance of his plays in Ireland for many years.

O'Casey also wrote poems, short stories, theatrical criticism and no less than six volumes of autobiography.

Although he continued as an active and not unsuccessful writer for the rest of his long life, his best work came out of his early years of struggle in Dublin. He'll always be remembered for his masterpiece, 'Juno and the Paycock', and for Boyle's prophetic and still accurate line. Today, as in Ireland in the twenties,

'Th' whole worl's in a terrible state o' chassis . . .'

Chapter Six

JAMES JOYCE
1882–1941

James Joyce was born in Dublin, into a big family with the traditional hard-working mum and charming, drunken dad. Joyce was a bright, rebellious boy from the very first and his father made sure he got a good education. In 1898 Joyce entered University College, Dublin, where he soon got into trouble for rejecting religious studies for the works of new European dramatists like Ibsen. In 1902 James Joyce left Dublin for Paris to study medicine. He enjoyed life in Paris but he had to return to Dublin when his mother became badly ill. After her death, Joyce divided his time between boozing with fellow medical students and struggling to get started as a writer.

Dublin Days

In Joyce's autobiographical novel 'Portrait of the Artist as a Young Man', Stephen Dedalus, like his creator, is sensitive, spindly, and short-sighted. He struggles with religious doubts, and sexual urges,

'Write it all down my son —
it could be a best seller!'

discovers art and literature, and has an almost mystical first-experience of sex with a young Dublin prostitute. Filled with guilt he repents and thinks of entering the priesthood. Finally he comes to realise that he can only find fulfilment as an artist, and decides to leave Dublin and go abroad to *'forge his soul.'* 'Portrait of the Artist' is a young man's book, redeemed by the clarity and vividness of the writing.

Abroad with Norah Barnacle

The time Joyce spent boozing in the Dublin pubs was to provide him with his greatest inspiration. On June 16th 1904 he met a barmaid with the splendid name of Norah Barnacle. They fell in love and the

'Ah you're pure genius Norah!'

following October they ran off together to Zurich. They stayed together for the rest of Joyce's life and married, a little belatedly in 1931 – they had two children by then. Throughout this time they lived on the Continent, first in Zurich and later in Trieste. Joyce carried on with his writing, supporting himself by working as an English teacher.

As well as 'Portrait of the Artist' Joyce produced a volume of poetry, and a book of short stories called 'Dubliners', about the frustrations of Irish life. But his real claims to fame are two massive experimental novels, 'Ulysses' and 'Finnegans Wake'.

Amazing Ulysses

The leading characters in 'Ulysses' are Leopold Bloom, a timid Jewish advertisement salesman, his voluptuous wife Molly – a character based firmly on Norah Barnacle – and Stephen Dedalus from 'Portrait of the Artist'. The novel's events all take place on one day in Dublin. The story moves through a public bath, a newspaper office, a library, several pubs, a maternity hospital, and a brothel, and introduces an amazing variety of Dublin themes and characters.

It uses a variety of styles and techniques from the good old 'stream of consciousness' through parody, realism, and fantasy. The one day in Dublin stands for all human life and Bloom, the archetypal 'little man', represents all mankind. Stephen, who he meets only at the end of the book, is the son he always wanted. The pattern of the book is loosely based on the 'Odyssey' by the classical Greek writer Homer.

Sexy Molly

'Ulysses' is an amazing work, rich, colourful, complicated and hilariously funny. Its publication caused an amazing amount of fuss. It was the naughty bits that caused all the trouble, particularly Molly Bloom's long sexy soliloquy at the end as she recalls the first time she made love:

> *'And I thought well as well him as another and then I asked him with my eyes to ask again yes and then he asked me would I yes to say yes my mountain flower and first I put my arms around him yes and drew him down to me so he could feel my breasts all perfume yes and his heart was going like mad and yes I said yes I will Yes.'*

'Read me Molly's sexy soliloquy...'

'No, No, no, no...!'

The book was published in Paris in 1922 without any trouble. (What would you expect from all those sex-mad frogs?) But the pure-minded New York post office authorities were so shocked that they burned the copies of the first English language edition. Not to be outdone, Folkstone customs officials seized the second edition in 1923. For the next thirteen years English readers had to make do with copies smuggled in from the sinful Continent. 'Ulysses' was finally published in England in 1936, and in America a year later.

Fantastic Finnegan

James Joyce's second epic is the even more fantastic 'Finnegans Wake', published in 1939. For this book Joyce created a language of his own, using puns, obscure allusions and made-up words. The book's opening words are:

'riverun, past Eve and Adam's, from swerve of shore to bend of bay brings us by a commodious vicus of recirculation, back to Howth Castle and Environs.'

Later on come such coinages as:

'All moanday, tearsday, wailsday, thumpsday, frightday, shatterday.'

Someone is described as having

'a base barreltone voice.'

While 'Ulysses' took place all in one day, 'Finnegans Wake' takes place all in one night – and all in the mind of a Dublin pub owner called Humphrey Chimpden Earwicker – HCE for short. The initials also stand for Here Comes Everybody. The novel's themes are the recurring cycles of man's universal history, and the inner life of the artist. 'Finnegans Wake' is an amazing eccentric achievement. You could call it the ultimate Irish joke. It was published to a baffled and angry reception, but today it's recognised as a uniquely original work of genius.

Hard Times for Joyce

An exile all his life, Joyce moved from place to place on the Continent, usually hard up. Much of his work was published in instalments in magazines and his reputation grew only very slowly. Joyce made very little money from his writing. From time to time better-off friends and patrons helped him out. James Joyce suffered constantly from poor eyesight and had to have a long series of eye operations. In addition he was constantly worried about the mental health of his daughter. She had a severe nervous breakdown in 1932, and was later diagnosed as an incurable schizophrenic. Eventually Joyce's own health gave way. He had surgery for a duodenal ulcer, and never really recovered. He died in 1941, and was buried in Zurich.

Portrait of the Artist

Now over fifty years after his death, the stubborn, short-sighted little Irishman is recognised as one of the world's greatest writers. 'Ulysses' in particular is an acknowledged masterpiece. Throughout all his struggles and hard times, James Joyce never gave up. He achieved what his character Stephen Dedalus set out to do, breaking free of the petty restrictions of nineteenth-century Dublin life, and forging his soul as an artist.

Chapter Seven

FRANK O'CONNOR
1903–1966

Short Story Superstar

Frank O'Connor wrote some of the famous short stories in Irish Lit – many of them several times over! He was such a perfectionist that he kept writing and re-writing his stories, never convinced he'd got them quite right. When the time came to make up story-collections,

'I've read these stories three times before.'

'I've written them three times before!'

most of the stories existed in several different versions. Frank O'Connor had the perfect solution. He used to sit down and write yet *another* version of each story, especially for the collection.

The Boy from Cork

Frank O'Connor was born in Cork in 1903, the son of a soldier. The family was far from well-off and young Frank didn't get much formal education – he left school when he was twelve. Nevertheless, he became a leading figure in Irish literature. He wrote a couple of novels, 'The Saint and Mary Kate' and 'Dutch Interior', and 'The Big Feller', a biography of the Irish leader Michael Collins. He also produced a good deal of poetry and criticism – but his real fame stems from his many short stories. (His real name was Michael O'Donovan but he used the O'Connor pen-name all his writing life.)

Fighting and Writing

Frank O'Connor grew up in the troubled years after the First World War, and soon became involved in the struggles for Irish freedom. In the Irish Civil War of 1922/23 he was jailed for 'Republican activities'. The experiences of this time feature largely in his first story collection, the ironically titled 'Guests of the Nation' published in 1931.

When the fighting died down the young revolutionary became a librarian. You might think he'd find it a bit dull, but in Ireland even the library service has its problems. Part of O'Connor's duties was the setting up of new libraries in the country districts of Ireland. This involved gaining the support of the parish priest – which wasn't always easy. In his autobiography, 'My Father's Son', O'Connor tells how one old priest obviously thought books were pretty dangerous things.

'You'll love the title – I'm calling it "Guests of the Nation".'

'Could we really thrust them into the hands of simple Irish country people?'

Dublin and The Abbey

O'Connor took a keen interest in drama, and shocked the citizens of Cork by putting on plays by such exotic foreign writers as Ibsen and Chekhov.

He also continued with his own writing. His first stories were written in Irish, and he translated a good deal of Irish poetry. He was encouraged by the Irish poet George Russell, known as Æ, and by a publisher called Harold Macmillan – who later became better-known as the Prime Minister of England.

Since he wrote vivid down-to-earth tales of everyday Irish life, O'Connor's own work was often judged far from innocuous, and he had his share of problems with the Establishment.

In one of his short stories, O'Connor pokes fun at his critics. 'The

Sorcerer's Apprentice'is about a young lady who is having doubts about marrying her boyfriend. O'Connor's easy relaxed style draws the reader straight into the story:

'If I have to propose to you many more times Una — I'll be the one with a slipped disc!'

> 'Their friends said that whenever Jimmy Foley named the day Una slipped a disc. For five years now they had been keeping company, and three times Una had slipped a disc . . .'

Una goes to stay with her married friend Joan Sheehy, so she can talk over her problems.

As the two girls lie in bed talking:

> 'Slowly the door opened, and Mick Sheehy, a tall man with a dark moustache, stumbled in. He was clutching a pillow as if it were a baby, his pyjamas were dangling about his crotch, and his eyes were closed. Joan jumped up and made room for him.
> "Lie there and keep quiet!" she said fiercely. "I'm not done talking to Una yet."
> "What are ye talking about?" he asked, wedging his shoulder comfortably into Una's hip. "Anything interesting?"
> "Only about herself and Jimmy."
> "Oh that!" he said with a noisy yawn and composed himself comfortably for sleep between the pair of them, his hands crossed piously on his stomach. Una, who was a well-read girl, wondered what Joan would say if any Irish writer reported a scene like that.'

Thanks largely to his collections of short stories, O'Connor's reputation grew steadily. He moved to Dublin, where he wrote reviews and articles for the 'Irish Statesman' and became one of the directors of the Abbey Theatre. In 1958 a row over censorship blew up. O'Connor resigned from the board of the Abbey Theatre in disgust. Like many another Irish exile before him, he took himself off to the United States.

He spent much of his remaining life in America, teaching for some years in an American university.

An Irish Chekhov

Frank O'Connor produced a number of short story collections – 'Bone of Contention', 'Crab Apple Jelly', 'The Common Chord', 'Traveller's Samples', 'My Oedipus Complex' and many more. His stories are full of humour, insight and compassion, and what he called 'the warm, dim, odorous, feckless, evasive southern quality' of his native Cork. He has been compared to the classic Russian short story writer Chekhov.

The Little Mother

'The Little Mother', for example, tells how Joan has to look after her father and two younger sisters when her mother dies. She becomes a tyrant and makes all
their lives a misery:

*'Kitty and May
soon realised they had lost a sister
and caught a tartar. Now she had
real authority and harried them
mercilessly, particularly poor Kitty
who had been untidy from birth and
left a litter of dirty clothes and
pots and pans behind her.'*

Joan drives away her handsome fiancé Dick, replacing him with shy, umbrella-carrying Chris. When May gets involved with a married man, Joan confronts him, gets back her sister's letters and breaks up the affair.

Next, Kitty leaves home and gets a job in another town. Before long she finds herself in trouble. Mick, their father, takes the news with philosophical calm.

'Ah, I can't be angry with the girl, Joanie. It was my own fault for letting her go to a strange town by herself. Sure, what is she, only a child?'

It's the outraged Joan who goes to see the guilty man, a dreamy mother-dominated student called Con, and bullies him into doing right by her sister.

Worn out by all this domestic drama, Joan turns to her shy fiancé Chris for consolation. Chris rises to the occasion.

'As a romantic lover, Chris was no great shakes, but he knew desperation when he saw it . . .'

Soon, Joan is in the same trouble as her sister. Chris is eager to marry her – but when Joan has to tell her father, she breaks down in self-reproach.

'I'm a liar and a hypocrite. I bullied you and I bullied the girls and ye have every reason to despise me . . .'

Her father tells her,

'I had the best wife the Lord God ever gave to a man and I treated her like a dog. I wake up in the middle of the night and think about it and cry and a hell of a lot of good that is to her or me! . . . If your mother is anywhere, she's here tonight, and what she has to say, I'm saying for her. We're proud of you, and we're delighted you're getting married.'

O'Connor packs enough family drama into this one short story for a long-running soap opera or a blockbusting family saga. In 'Private Property' O'Connor makes fun of his youth as a dedicated revolutionary:

'My mother was never really happy about my being in the secret revolutionary army, and Father hated it . . . He tried to keep me in check by making me be home at ten, but I felt that as a revolutionist, as well as a wage earner, I had to hold out for half past.'

Frank O'Connor depicted the everyday life of the ordinary people of Ireland in hundreds of brilliant short stories. Perhaps the distinguished writer and critic V.S. Pritchett summed up his achievement best.

'It has often been said that Ireland is packed with genius but is short on talent. Frank O'Connor was one of a distinguished generation who had both.'

Chapter Eight

SAMUEL BECKETT
1906–1989

Good Things in Small Parcels

There's an old saying about good things coming in small parcels – and that certainly applies to the writings of Samuel Beckett. Some writers produce millions of words and still sink without trace. Sam Beckett managed to make an enormous reputation with two slim volumes of poetry, one book of short stories, five short novels and a handful of even shorter plays. (One of his later plays, called 'Breath', lasts only thirty seconds.) There's no doubt about it, size isn't everything . . .

'That Beckett play we've just watched was shorter than the Commercials!'

Prize Pupil

For a rather eccentric writer, Beckett's beginnings were normal enough. He was born near Dublin, the son of a quantity surveyor. As a lad he was good at games *and* schoolwork and ended up at Trinity College, Dublin, where he studied French and Italian Literature. Still keen on sport, especially cricket, he toured England with the university cricket team in 1927. He did well in his studies too. Not only did he get a first class degree, he actually came first in his year. His reward was a post as an exchange lecturer at the Ecole Normale Supérieure in Paris.

Beckett Abroad

Beckett soon found he didn't really enjoy teaching. He started playing his pupils Wagner when he ought to have been teaching them English. But he enjoyed being in France. Paris in the twenties, he said later, was 'a good place for a young man to be'. It was the intellectual centre of Europe in those days, the birthplace of all the latest literary and artistic ideas. It was also the home of a lively circle of expatriate writers and artists like Hemingway, Scott Fitzgerald and Gertrude Stein. Young Sam started mixing in artistic circles. He met and made friends with a fellow Irish exile, the famous James Joyce. For a time Beckett acted as a sort of assistant, occasionally taking down chunks of 'Finnegan's Wake' to Joyce's dictation. One day when Joyce was dictating someone knocked on the door.

Joyce shouted 'Come in!' – and Beckett wrote it down!

When Joyce read over his dictation, he asked why two extra words had been added to his masterpiece.

'Well, you said it!' replied Beckett.

Joyce thought it over, then said loftily, 'Let it stand!'

Home and Away

In 1930 Beckett had to go home to Dublin to take up his post as an assistant lecturer at Trinity College. He was all set for a brilliant career as an Irish academic. But he didn't like teaching Irish students any more than he did French ones. He said it was absurd trying to teach other people when he felt he didn't really know anything himself. He missed the intellectual freedom of France as well. On a sudden impulse he resigned his safe university job to become a writer.

Wandering Sam

Beckett's life was pretty unsettled for the next few years, as he wandered restlessly round Ireland, France and Germany. Luckily he had a small legacy, enough to keep him alive. He published two volumes of poetry, a volume of short stories, 'More Pricks than Kicks', and a novel, 'Murphy', about a tormented loner who dies just as he finds contentment. None of them made much impact, or earned him much money.

Beckett at War

When war broke out in 1939, Beckett was back at home, visiting

Dublin. Most people would have considered this a lucky escape, but not Sam Beckett. He set straight off for war-torn France and joined the French resistance. In 1942 he left occupied Paris one jump ahead of the Gestapo, and spent the rest of the war in hiding in the South of France, disguised as a farm labourer, and writing another novel, 'Watt', to pass the time. At the end of the war he was awarded the Croix de Guerre for his courageous work for the resistance.

With the war over, Beckett returned to Paris to resume his career as a writer. He wrote three more novels, 'Molloy', 'Malone Dies' and 'The Unnamable'. All three took the form of bleak interior monologues. The last one ends:

> *'Where I am I don't know, I'll never know, in the silence you don't know, you must go on, I can't go on, I'll go on.'*

It's the characteristic Beckett message.

The Astonishing Godot

Feeling he had exhausted the possibilities of the novel, Beckett turned to the theatre. In 1953 there came the Paris première of the play that made Samuel Beckett famous – 'Waiting for Godot'.

The setting is an open plain, with a little mound on which grows a tatty tree. A tramp, Estragon, sits on the mound, trying to pull off his boot. Another tramp, Vladimir, wanders on, and there's some vague and desultory chat. Estragon suggests they leave. *'We can't,'* says Vladimir. *'We're waiting for Godot.'* Two more characters appear. The fat and pompous Pozzo leads the miserable luggage-laden Lucky by a rope round his neck. Pozzo enjoys a picnic, the others hang around and wrangle. A Boy appears. *'Godot won't come this evening,'* he tells them.

'But surely tomorrow . . .'

The second act is pretty much the same. Pozzo and Lucky reappear, Pozzo now mysteriously blind. The Boy reappears too, telling them, *'Godot will come tomorrow without fail.'*

Vladimir and Estragon decide to hang themselves from the tree. They test the rope holding up Estragon's trousers, but it breaks and they almost fall. They decide to come back tomorrow with a better bit of rope. After all, says Vladimir, if Godot doesn't come to save them, they can still hang themselves. He suggests they go. Estragon agrees. Nobody moves. That's it. As one despairing critic said, "'Waiting for Godot' is a play in which nothing happens – twice!"

'I'm waiting for Godot!'

Beckett's Message

As in his novels, Beckett's message seems to be one of bleak despair. Life is miserable, futile and, above all, ambiguous. No-one knows what's going to happen, no-one even knows what's going on now. It's impossible to know what to do for the best, or even if it's worth doing anything. Godot may, or may not, be God. He may punish the two tramps, or save them. He may never even come at all . . . The really astonishing thing – and you won't believe until you see it – is that on the stage, Beckett's play makes this miserable message exciting, dramatic and often hilariously funny!

Beckett gets Tough

After a lifetime of poverty and obscurity, the success of 'Godot' brought Beckett world-wide fame. He didn't enjoy it – he said he felt more comfortable with failure!

In his later plays, Beckett struggles, almost perversely, to do more and more with less and less, making fewer and fewer concessions, forcing his audiences to work ever harder. 'Endgame' is a one-act play about Hamm, who is blind, his servant Clov' and Hamm's old parents who spend the day in two dustbins! In 'Krapp's Last Tape' an embittered old man listens to tapes of his younger self.

In 'Happy Days' Winnie, the main character, stays obstinately cheerful, despite being buried up to her waist in a mound of rubbish. (Her husband, the other character, seems a bit fed up.)

'Come and Go' has three female characters who move about the stage muttering inaudibly, performing some mysterious ritual, and a text that's just over a hundred words long. 'Breath', the thirty-second play mentioned earlier, consists of a pile of rubbish, a breath and a cry. (No worries about catching the last bus home!)

'Not I' is a brief, confused monologue in which all we see on stage is the actor's (or actress's, who knows?) spotlit mouth . . . Beckett also wrote a number of plays for radio and television, and he published his 'Collected Poems' in 1971.

Beckett's Success

Samuel Beckett was a success in spite of himself. he fought hard to stay a failure, but it was no use. After 'Waiting for Godot' he just couldn't do anything wrong. The shorter and more difficult he made his works, the more critics and audiences lapped them up. He could have put a spit and a cough on stage and had a hit. Despite all his best efforts, he ended his days as a much-revered literary figure, a leading light of the Theatre of the Absurd, an influence on such playwrights as Harold Pinter and Tom Stoppard. Just to rub it in, they gave him the Nobel Prize. No one ever did better out of misery, gloom and despair . . .

Chapter Nine

FLANN O'BRIEN
1911–1966

A Man of Many Names

Flann O'Brien's real name was Brian O'Nolan, or sometimes O'Nuillan. He was also Miles na Gopaleen, Lir O'Connor, and quite a few others as well.

Brian O'Nolan (to stick with that name for the moment) was born in Strabane, Co. Tyrone, third child in a family of twelve. He was the son of a Customs Officer, whose work took him all over Ireland. Irish was spoken at home, and the boy was discouraged from playing with other children, in case he got into the bad habit of speaking English! He was educated at Blackrock College where he led a campaign against the compulsory wearing of blazers made in

'Hate to worry you old chap but— Flan O'Brien's creeping up on you!'

Britain, writing 'Burn British Blazers' in big letters on the school wall. He went on to University College, Dublin, where he studied Irish, German and Philosophy.

He also edited student magazines, won medals for public speaking, and gained a reputation as the college wit. He began writing too, and early drafts of his novels 'At Swim-Two-Birds' and 'The Third Policeman' were written in his student days.

A Respectable Civil Servant

In 1935 Brian O'Nolan entered the Irish Civil Service. For a while he was too busy to think about writing. But when his father died unexpectedly in 1937, the large family was left hard up. Brian decided to see if he could earn himself a bit extra by writing. He revised 'At Swim-Two-Birds' and sent it off to various publishers. It was accepted by Longman, largely on the basis of an enthusiastic report from their reader – a fellow called Graham Greene. The novel was published in 1939 under the pen-name Flann O'Brien. Writing novels wasn't considered a proper occupation for a respectable Irish Civil Servant. O'Nolan was paid an advance of thirty pounds, which didn't exactly solve his financial problems . . .

(Incidentally, there's a story that O'Nolan and his friends sometimes raised the wind by selling battered old black felt hats to rich American tourists – with the solemn assurance that the hats had been worn by the great James Joyce himself . . .)

'At Swim-Two-Birds'

'At Swim-Two-Birds' is a wildly experimental novel, much influenced by Joyce, which works on several levels. Partly a comic, realistic picture of student life, it also contains a 'novel within a novel', about the legendary Irish hero Finn Mac Cool, and some farcical Irish folklore.

Reviews were good, if a bit baffled, and Dylan Thomas called it a masterpiece. A copy even reached Sam Beckett in Paris. He showed it to James Joyce who called it 'a really funny book'.

But despite all this high-powered endorsement, the book didn't sell all that well. Most of the remaining copies were lost when Longman's warehouse was bombed at the beginning of World War Two.

O'Brien and Sexton Blake

Still hard up, O'Brien was reduced to writing Sexton Blake stories at fifty pounds a go. Encouraged by the experience, he decided to try a thriller of his own. He wrote a satirically intellectual detective novel called 'The Third Policeman' – and was shattered when it was rejected for publication. Pure chance, or maybe the luck of the Irish, was soon to come to his aid.

Miles Funnier

For some time, Brian O'Nolan had been contributing to a witty correspondence in the columns of the 'Irish Times' about the merits, or otherwise, of a play by Frank O'Connor. The editor was amused by his letters, and asked to meet him. The meeting led to O'Nolan being asked to write a humorous column for the paper. Written at first in Irish, then alternately in Irish and English, and finally mostly in English, the column appeared under the name of Miles na Gopaleen. It ran in the 'Irish Times' for the next twenty-seven years.

From the very first the column attracted letters of protest – and letters of praise as well. Ranging over a wide variety of Dublin and Irish life it established a number of running jokes including the opinions of 'The Brother', the kind of know-it-all to be found in every Dublin bar.

'The brother has it all worked out, how we can get through the war . . . we all go to bed for a week, every month. Cripples, drunks, policemen, watchmen – everybody. Nobody is allowed to be up . . . Do you see, when nobody is up you save clothes, shoes, rubber, petrol, coal, turf, timber and everything we're short of. And food too, remember. Because tell me this – what makes you hungry? It's work that makes you hungry . . . Stop in bed and all you'll ask is an odd slice of bread . . .'

Then there were Keats and Chapman, whose rambling adventures always ended in an excruciating pun. Hearing how school bullies had once glued the young Chapman to his headmaster, Keats remarked, *'I like a man that sticks to his principles.'* Chasing an escaped steed high and low, Keats announced that he was *'dogging a fled horse'*.

Finding a young friend in his workshop manufacturing fake half crowns Chapman said, *'He is making excellent progress.'* *'He is forging ahead,'* agreed Keats.

It grows on you after a time . . .

With the column established, O'Nolan moved on to other writing. He wrote another novel, a satire on the Irish language movement called 'The Poor Mouth'. He wrote a play, 'Faustus Kelly', which had a modest success at the Abbey Theatre, and his translation of Kapek's 'The Insect World' was performed at the Gaiety Theatre.

He was still working in the Civil Service, and in 1948 he married Evelyn McDonnell, who worked in the typing pool. His friends expressed surprise that any girl would take on Miles na Gopaleen – but it was a long and happy marriage which lasted for the rest of his life.

'Do you, Brian O'Nolan, O'Nuillan, Miles na Gopaleen, Lir O'Connor, Flann O'Brien, take this woman....'

The Uncivil Servant

But if his writing and his private life were prospering, Brian O'Nolan's official career wasn't doing nearly so well. Never a dedicated Civil Servant, he grew increasingly bored with his job. Like many another writer, he was fond of a drink or two or three. He was occasionally known to turn up for meetings somewhat the worse for wear.

What's more, his Miles na Gopaleen column was taking on a sharper more political tone, and important feathers were being ruffled . . .

Things came to a head, and in 1953 he was more or less forcibly retired 'on medical grounds' – and given a magnificent four pounds a week pension. He tried to make up his lost salary by more writing, but despite the success of the column, more work was hard to come by. O'Nolan began to feel that both his careers were now over.

Once again, luck came to his aid.

A Writer Re-born

In 1959 a young publisher wrote to him from London, saying he had long admired the now forgotten 'At Swim-Two-Birds' and would like to re-publish it. The book was re-issued in 1960 – to an enthusiastic welcome. Flattering comparisons were made to the great James Joyce. Flann O'Brien was a success again!

Much encouraged, O'Nolan set to work on another novel, 'The Hard Life'. In the following years, several of his plays were produced on television.

He wrote a smash-hit series of fifteen-minute comedies for the Irish comedian Jimmy O'Dea, and another novel, 'The Dalkey Archive', a satirical comedy about James Joyce living secretly in a sea-side town outside Dublin. Published in 1964, it was another great success, and was adapted for the stage by the famous Irish playwright Hugh Leonard, under the title of 'The Saints Go Cycling In'. Even 'The Brother' found his way onto the stage in a one-man show.

The Final Chapter

Although he was only in his mid-fifties, Brian O'Nolan's health was beginning to fail, worn out by a life of hard writing and hard drinking. He died suddenly in 1966 – on April 1st. When the news came out, lots of peple thought it was another of Miles na Gopaleen's jokes.

Strangely enough there was one more joke to come, the best of all.

His publisher expressed interest in any surviving unpublished work.
Brian's wife Evelyn sent him the manuscript of the long-ago rejected

novel, 'The Third Policeman'. It was published in 1967 to great
acclaim. Many consider it to be his masterpiece. Brian O'Nolan,
Flann O'Brien, Miles na Gopaleen – Ireland's greatest humorist had
managed to have the last laugh . . .

Chapter Ten

BRENDAN BEHAN
1923–1964

A Broth of a Bhoy

Brendan Behan did more than most to create the myth of the writer as wild man, reeling round the bars of Dublin, full of poetry, rebellion and Guinness. It was a role he greatly enjoyed and he spent most of his life playing it to the hilt. But beneath all the bluster and blarney, he was a talented and sensitive writer.

Brendan the Rebel

Life plunged Behan into trouble from an early age. He was born in the tenements of Dublin, the child of a well-read and staunchly Republican family. Behan was keener on revolution than on reading. At the ripe age of fourteen he joined the I.R.A. Two years later he was over in Liverpool, with a suitcase full of explosives.

Brendan himself describes what came next in his book 'Borstal Boy':

'Friday, in the evening, the landlady shouted up the stairs: "Oh God, oh Jesus, oh Sacred Heart. Boy, there's two gentlemen to see you."

'I knew by the screeches of her that these two gentlemen were not calling to inquire about my health, or to know if I'd had a good trip. I grasped my suitcase containing Pot, Chlor, Sulph Ac, gelignite, detonators, electrical and ignition, and the rest of my Sinn Fein conjurors outfit, and carried it to the window. Then the gentlemen arrived.

'A young one with a blond Herrenvolk head and a BBC accent shouted, "I say, greb him, the bestud."'

And greb him they did.

Brendan in Borstal

Because of his youth – he was still only sixteen – Brendan escaped prison. He was sentenced to three years in Borstal – an 'approved school' or special training establishment for young offenders.

Brendan coped with Borstal pretty well. Conditions were hard – but no harder than the tenement life he was used to. (He was amazed when they issued him with a pair of pyjamas – he'd never had any before.)

Released a year early, he was deported back to Ireland in 1941.

Brendan in Jail

He didn't stay out of trouble for very long. In April of the following year there was a demonstration in Glasnevin Cemetery, Dublin, to commemorate the Easter Rising of 1916. Brendan was arrested again – and subsequently sentenced to fourteen years for shooting at a policeman. (Luckily, he didn't hit him.) Less than a year after leaving a British Borstal, Brendan was locked up in an Irish prison. It was here, with plenty of time and very few distractions, that he first started writing. His first published story, 'I became a Borstal Boy', was actually written in Mountjoy Prison.

Once again Brendan's luck was in. After serving only four of his fourteen years, he was released in the post-war amnesty of 1946.

In Trouble – and in Print

Brendan led a pretty varied life for the next few years. He worked, on and off, as a house painter, went to sea for a while, and tried his hand at a bit of smuggling. He did a few months in Strangeways for trying to free an I.R.A. prisoner from an English jail, and a month's hard labour in Mountjoy Prison for assaulting a policeman. (He said the sight of police uniforms upset him.) By now he was building a career as a freelance journalist. In 1953 his first novel 'The Scarperer' was serialised in the Irish Times. A year later, he was producing a regular column in the Irish Press. And he was writing a play . . .

The Quare Fellow

Brendan Behan's play, 'The Quare Fellow', first opened at the Pike Theatre in Dublin. But it was the later London production, directed by the dynamic Joan Littlewood, that brought him fame and fortune. The play is set in prison – Brendan was putting his hard-won experience to good use. 'The Quare Fellow' of the title is to be executed for murdering his wife. He never actually appears in the play. We see only the reactions of the prisoners, and the warders, to the coming execution. The play starts with a song:

> 'A hungry feeling came over me stealing
> And the mice were squealing in my prison cell.
> And that old triangle
> Went jingle jangle
> Along the banks of the Royal Canal . . .'

(Brendan was fond of using songs in his plays. He often joined in the singing from his place in the front stalls.)

Tension mounts in the prison as execution time approaches, affecting warders as much as prisoners. One warder bursts out:

'I think the whole show should be put on in Croke Park; after all it's at the public expense and they let it go on.

They should have something more for their money than a bit of paper stuck on a gate.'

The whole play is a brilliant black comedy – and a savage depiction of the horror of capital punishment.

The Hostage

The success of the play made Brendan Behan a celebrity, and he played the role with great enthusiasm. He appeared in pubs, at literary parties and on television, invariably in a state of cheerful intoxication. But somehow, between drinks, he was working as well.

He followed 'The Quare Fellow' with another play, 'The Hostage'. Set in a Dublin brothel, it tells of the last few hours in the life of a young English soldier. He is being held hostage for the life of a young I.R.A. man in prison. If the Irish boy is executed, he will die too.

Even wilder and more outrageous than 'The Quare Fellow', the play fills the stage with a cast of drunks, prostitutes, perverts, pimps and dedicated revolutionaries. The uproarious action is broken up with more than twenty songs. One critic said Brendan Behan didn't

'Remember the good old days, when Brendan was alive – we could always get a part in one of his plays.'

so much open up the stage as kick it to bits. Yet, just as with 'The Quare Fellow', the basic theme is tragically serious. The young

51

English soldier, a nice, dim Cockney lad, knows nothing of the history of Ireland. He doesn't understand why he's there, or why he is to be shot.

'But I ain't done nothing!' he cries pathetically.
'You are the hostage,' he is told. *'This is war.'*

Borstal Memories

In the same year, Behan published 'Borstal Boy'. The third, and many believe the finest, of his major works, it's a sensitively written account of his early imprisonment. We see the sixteen-year-old Brendan coping with the horrors of remand in Walton Jail, where prisoners slash each other with razors and he is beaten up by brutal warders. The most remarkable thing about the book is its good humour and lack of bitterness. Brendan writes almost nostalgically about the 'open Borstal' at Hollesley Bay to which he is transferred. He finds good mates, stars in the school show, and even wins an essay prize. Never a good hater, Brendan finds himself developing a kind of liking for some of his English enemies. When he's released, the sergeant who arrested him says, 'They've made a fine man of you, Brendan!'

Brendan's End

BRENDAN'S NEW YORK

After 'Borstal Boy' Brendan Behan produced only minor works like 'Brendan Behan's Ireland' and 'Brendan Behan's New York', rambling, lightweight travel books cashing in on his fame. Inevitably, the money, the fame, and above all, the booze finished him off in the end. His plays were successful in England, in America and in Europe, with Brendan rampaging along the celebrity trail after them. His health started to give way, but he refused to slow down. Urged by friends to be more careful he roared, 'Bigod, I'd sooner be dead than think about dying!' Brendan Behan died in Meath Hospital in Dublin, forty-one years old. It had been a fairly short life, but a very merry one – and it had produced at least three works of literature.

At the end of 'The Hostage' the dead soldier jumps up and joins in the play's final chorus:

'The bells of hell
Go ting-a-ling-a-ling
For you but not for me
Oh death where is thy sting-a-ling-a-ling
Or grave thy victory?'

There was so much life and energy in Brendan Behan, that you can almost see him doing the same!

Chapter Eleven

EDNA O'BRIEN
1932–

Edna O'Brien, happily still with us, is a stunning green-eyed redhead who rapidly became famous, even notorious, for the lyricism of her prose and the frankness of her novels. Born in the West of Ireland, she was educated at the Convent of Mercy at Loughrea, County Galway, and later attended the Pharmaceutical College in Dublin. She was married at 20, divorced thirteen years later, and has two sons. Edna O'Brien has lived in London ever since 1959. Like many other writers, she felt she had to leave Ireland to write about it properly.

The Country Girls

Edna O'Brien's first novel, 'The Country Girls', was published in 1959. First of a trilogy, it tells of the lives and loves of Kate and Baba, one shy and romantic, the other outgoing and cynical. Kate, who tells the story, has a schoolgirl romance with the romantic, mysterious – and married – 'Mr Gentleman'.

Young Love

'He kissed me. It was a real kiss.
It affected my entire body. My
toes, though they were numb and
pinched in the new shoes, responded
to that kiss, and for a few minutes
my soul was lost. Then I felt a
drop on the end of my nose and
it bothered me. "Blue Noses," I
said, looking for my handkerchief.
"What are Blue Noses?" he asked.
"The name for winter roses," I said . . .
On the way back he had to get out
a few times because the windshield wipers
were choked up. Even for the second he was away I was lonesome for him.'

So that's why I feel it in my toes when you kiss me!

After a few more stolen meetings, Mr Gentleman goes abroad, and the romance is over . . .

Off to Dublin

Three years later, Kate and Baba leave their convent school and escape to Dublin. Baba is to take a commercial course, Kate to work in a grocery shop. Kate is still pining for Mr Gentleman, but the more practical Baba fixes up a date with two wealthy older men.

> ' "We want to live. Drink gin. Squeeze into the front of big cars and drive up to big hotels."
> "But we want young men. Romance. Love and things," I said despondently. I thought of standing under a streetlamp in the rain with my hair falling crazily about, my lips poised for the miracle of a kiss. A kiss, nothing more. My imagination did not go beyond that . . .'

Mr Gentleman reappears and he and Kate renew their romance. They arrange to go away together, but on the eve of departure comes a telegram:

Mr Gentleman reappears

'EVERYTHING GONE WRONG. THREATS FROM YOUR FATHER. MY WIFE HAS ANOTHER NERVOUS BREAKDOWN . . . MUST NOT SEE YOU.'

The Lonely Girl

In 'The Lonely Girl' Kate, who's obviously a glutton for punishment, falls for another older, married man, a film director called Eugene. They begin an affair, which her furious family try to break up in a scene of farcical violence. Eugene decides he's too old for her, everything ends unhappily, and Kate leaves for England with Baba . . .

Married Bliss

The third book, 'Girls in Their Married Bliss', is partly narrated by Baba. She and Kate are both married now –

> 'bemoaning the fact that nothing would ever improve, that we'd die the way we were – enough to eat, married, dissatisfied.'

Kate has re-met and married her Eugene, Baba has the rich husband she's always wanted, an Irish builder called Frank. Neither of them are happy. Baba can't seem to have children with Frank, so

she has a quick fling with a drummer and gets pregnant. Outraged at first, Frank eventually forgives her.

Kate meets and falls for someone else – married of course. Her marriage breaks up and she loses both husband and child.

Sad Epilogue

In a brief epilogue, set some years later, the exasperated Baba tells how Kate continued her doomed quest for love.

'I knew there was some bloody man and that he was probably married and that she saw him once a fortnight or less, but of course saw him in street lamps, rain puddles and all that kind of Lord Byron lunacy. This was the real thing, it was different from all the rest, he and she were meant, Tristan and Iseult . . .'

Yet Baba half-envies her hopelessly romantic friend.

> 'I was livid with her on two counts: first of all, why should she be having this goddam, occasional illicit ecstasy when I have to settle for a boring life . . . and secondly why couldn't she see reason, why couldn't she see that people are brigands, what made her think there was such a thing as twin-star perpetuity, when all around her people were scraping for bits of happiness and not getting anywhere . . .'

Kate's ever-hopeful but ultimately tragic life ends in suicide. At the end of the book Baba, battered by life but surviving, is on her way to her friend's funeral . . .

Edna O'Brien is often identified with Kate, if only because of her red hair and green eyes. Unlike her unhappy heroine, she survived to write many more books – though happiness still tends to elude her always-female leading characters.

More Love and Grief

'August is a Wicked Month' and 'Casualties of Peace' both tell of women whose marriages have broken down. Like Kate, they never quite give up the search for love and happiness. 'A Pagan Place' tells of the Irish childhood of a girl who becomes a nun. Mary Hooligan, the lusty indomitable heroine of 'Night', has been compared to the Molly Bloom of James Joyce's 'Ulysses'. 'I Hardly Knew You' tells the story of a woman in prison for killing her younger lover – still no danger of a happy ending! It's fair to say that one theme runs through all Edna O'Brien's fiction – the search for love, never really successful, but never to be abandoned while life lasts.

'And now it's time for another unhappy love story, by Edna O'Brien...'

Stories and Screenplays

Edna O'Brien has also written short stories and screenplays, and edited a prose collection, 'Some Irish Loving'. Her non-fiction work includes 'Mother Ireland' and 'James and Nora', a study of the relationship of James Joyce and his wife.

As with many writers the success of her early works still overshadows all the rest. Her best loved characters will always be Kate and Baba, 'The Country Girls' who come to Dublin, full of youthful hopes, in search of love and life . . .

Chapter Twelve

SEAMUS HEANEY
1939–

The Country Boy

One of Ireland's, indeed one of the world's leading modern poets, Seamus Heaney has his roots firmly in Ireland's soil. The son of a farmer and cattle dealer, it's been said that mud features largely in his poetry!

Don't you dare go into the living-room Seamus, you've got poetry all over your shoes!

Born in Mossbawm, County Down, the eldest of nine children, he and his family were Catholics in a mainly Protestant area. Seamus won a scholarship to St Columb's College in Londonderry. From there he went on to Queen's University, Belfast, graduating with First Class Honours. Poetry was always the main passion of his life. In the sixties he was one of a lively group of young poets in Belfast, led by Phillip Hobsbaum, a lecturer at Queen's . . . They used, he said, 'to talk about poetry, day after day, with . . . intensity and prejudice!'

Poet's Progress

Even poets have to earn a living somehow and in 1962, Seamus

Heaney became an English teacher in a secondary school in Belfast. Between 1963 and 1966 he taught at St Thomas's College. In 1966 he was offered a lectureship at Queen's University, where he lectured in poetry for six years.

Seamus Heaney has lectured at Harvard University, and was guest lecturer at the University of California in 1970. In 1976 he moved to Dublin, as a lecturer in a Catholic College of Education. In 1989 he became Professor of Poetry at Oxford.

The Land

The experiences of his youth contributed one of his major themes – the land, on which his family had lived and worked for generations. An old saying tells us you can take the man out of the bog, but not the bog out of the man. Seamus Heaney loves and treasures his bogs, and makes good use of them in his poetry.

'They've taken the skeleton
Of the Great Irish Elk
Out of the peat, set it up
An astounding crate full of air.

Butter sunk under
More than a hundred years
Was recovered, salty and white.
The ground itself is kind, black butter.'

Picture of a Great Irish Elk in the bog.

In 'The Tollund Man' he compares a body preserved in the peat to all those who have died in Ireland in later years.

'If you're going to the bog, put clean underwear on —you might get preserved!'

'*Some day I will go to Aarhus*
To see his peat-brown head
The mild pods of his eye-lids,
His pointed skin cap.

I could risk blasphemy
Consecrate the cauldron bog
Our holy ground and pray
Him to make germinate

The scattered, ambushed
Flesh of labourers,
Stockinged corpses
Laid out in the farmyards . . .'

In 'Punishment' the poet grieves for a long-dead girl, her preserved body found in the bog.

'Mud should do my complexion a world of good.'

'Little adulteress
Before they punished you

you were flaxen haired,
undernourished, and your
tar-black face was beautiful.
My poor scapegoat . . .'

Childhood memories are another important part of his poetry. In 'Clearances' the poet, at his mother's deathbed, remembers how they peeled potatoes together when he was small.

'Er, thanks Mum – a potato knife!'

'Cold comforts set between us, things to share
Gleaming in a bucket of clean water
And again let fall. Little pleasant splashes
From each other's work would bring us to our senses.

So while the parish priest at her bedside
Went hammer and tongs at the prayers for the dying.
I remembered her head bent toward my head
Her breath in mine, our fluent dipping knives –
Never closer the whole rest of our lives.'

Nor does Seamus Heaney avoid the darker side of Irish life. In 'Casualty' he mourns for a friend, an old fisherman who became an innocent victim of the troubles.

'*He was blown to bits*
Out drinking in a curfew
Others obeyed, three nights
After they shot dead
The thirteen men in Derry.'

Another friend, a happy-go-lucky hippy type, is remembered in 'A Postcard from North Antrim'.

'*Drop-out on a come-back*
Prince of no-man's-land
With your head in clouds or sand,
You were the clown
Social worker of the town
Until your candid forehead stopped
A pointblank teatime bullet.'

Seamus Heaney's apparently simple, yet densely concentrated poetry has its roots deep in Irish soil and in Irish history, linking bodies long-preserved in peat to the troubles of today. His richly-textured verse recalls the experiences of his country childhood, and preserves their importance.

In one of his most characteristic poems, 'The Harvest Bow', a knot of corn woven by his father becomes full of significance.

'"The end of art is peace"
Could be the motto of this frail device
That I have pinned on the deal dresser
Like a drawn snare
Slipped lately by the spirit of the corn
Yet burnished by its passage and still warm . . .'